MW01600516

COVER HIM

Strategic Prayers for Your Future Spouse

FALICIA JONES MCKARRY

Dedicated to Ethan, Marley, and Melody.

ACKNOWLEDGEMENTS

THANK YOU MOM: For always believing in me, for always encouraging me, and always challenging me. You are the reason I am the mother, poet, writer, daughter, niece, sister and friend I am today. I love you and miss you. Until we meet again, I will continue making you proud!

TABLE OF CONTENTS

CHAPTER 1

BRING ON THE INCREASE

Affirmation: "My husband will display wisdom over our finances"

A Prayer for My Husband's Finances

Lord, I lift up my future husband's finances to you right now in the name of Jesus. Lord, I pray that even now, you begin to give him wisdom and stewardship over his money, credit and investments. Lord, because I know that if he can be a good steward over his finances now, then he will be an even better steward over our finances. Lord, I pray for an increase in his financial situation right now. Lord, increase his salary to his heart's desires. Lord, I pray that as you increase his portion, he will increase your portion. Lord, I pray for my husband's heart towards tithing. Give him biblical confirmation regarding what your word says about paying the tithe. Lord, give him wisdom in the area of sowing seeds. I pray

1

over the seeds he has sown thus far into charity, businesses, and ministries. I pray that they fall on good grounds God. Lord, I pray that you begin to water every seed right now, one by one Lord. I pray that you give him fresh ideas regarding his financial future, and how to secure the financial wellness he desires. I ask all these things in Jesus' name, Amen.

Verse: *"For the Lord your God will bless you as he has promised, and you will lend to many nations, but will borrow from none. You will rule over many nations, but none will rule over you." (Deuteronomy 15:6 NIV)*

COVER HIM

_____

_____

_____

_____

_____

_____

_____

_____

_____

_____

_____

_____

_____

_____

_____

_____

_____

_____

_____

_____

_____

_____

_____

_____

_____

_____

_____

_____

_____

_____

_____

_____

_____

_____

_____

COVER HIM

_____

_____

_____

_____

_____

_____

_____

_____

_____

_____

_____

_____

_____

_____

_____

_____

_____

_____

CHAPTER 2

GUIDE HIS FOOTSTEPS

*Affirmation: "My husband will dominate
and grow exponentially in his career"*

A Prayer for My Husband's Career

Lord, I just want to say thank you for my husband's career. I pray that you allow the anointing that you have placed on his life to flow through him on his job, when he interacts with his co-workers, and when his boss challenges him. I pray that his temperament remains calm, even under pressure. Lord, I ask that if there is any division on his job that you remove and replace as you see fit. Guide him, protect him and his work, in the name of Jesus. Lord, I speak travelling grace over him as he commutes daily to and from work. I pray no weapon formed against him on his job will prosper in the name of Jesus. Lord, if there be any anxiety, fear, or frustration about where he is right now in his career, I pray that it is replaced with peace and clarity right now. Guide him in the area of decision making. Lord, let him know that promotion belongs to you, which makes promotion *his* portion, elevation is *his* portion, and entrepreneurship is *his* portion. Allow him to elevate, whether it is on this job or in his own business. I pray that wherever he plants His feet, let them be guided by you, in Jesus' name, Amen.

Verse: *"The Lord will make you the head, not the tail. If you pay attention to the commands of the Lord your God that I give you this day and carefully follow them, you will always be at the top, never at the bottom. (Deuteronomy 28:13 NIV)*

COVER HIM

COVER HIM

CHAPTER 3

MAKE HIM WHOLE

Affirmation: "My husband is whole."

A Prayer for My Husband's Insecurities

Dear God, I would not be a good wife if I did not pray for the things my husband may never reveal to me. Lord, I pray that I can be a safe place for my husband to share his fears, worries, frustrations, and insecurities, whether about our (future) marriage, himself, or me. I cover him right now so that he will know that he is enough. Lord, let him know that his past does not define him, and neither will it determine his future. Lord remind him of his worth in you. God, let him know that you have graced him with forgiveness, worth, value, purpose, and anointing. Lord, I also pray for my husband's pride; teach me how to protect it and to never make him feel less than a man. I also pray that my husband doesn't allow his pride to overshadow the position and purpose you have set aside for him. I speak against egotistical and narcissistic traits of the enemy that are trying to subdue your people. I pray that my husband can effectively communicate his insecurities to me, and not try to hide behind one of those spirits. Lord, I cancel every assignment of the enemy that has tried to devalue my husband's worth. Let him know that just like you see him Lord, I see him too! Teach me how to comfort and nurture his insecurities while also empowering him in the areas that he may feel inadequate. Allow every tool, strategy, and resource that you have given him to come forth and remind him there's value in him and the world needs what he has. I ask these things in Jesus' name, Amen.

Verse: *"But now, this is what the Lord says, he who created Jacob, he who formed you, Israel: Do not fear, for I have redeemed you; I have called you by name; you are mine."* *(Isaiah 43:1 NIV)*

COVER HIM

_____

_____

_____

_____

_____

_____

_____

_____

_____

_____

_____

_____

_____

_____

_____

_____

_____

_____

_____

_____

_____

_____

_____

_____

_____

_____

_____

_____

_____

_____

_____

_____

_____

_____

_____

_____

_____

CHAPTER 4

YOU CALLED HIM HEALED

*Affirmation: "My husband has
a sound mind."*

A Prayer for My Husband's Mental Health

Lord, cover my husband in the name of Jesus. I speak against depression right now. Depression, flee right now in the name of Jesus! I speak against anxiety God, and I pray that he knows he can cast all of his cares onto you; for you care for him. Lord, lift every burden right now and take the shackles of bondage off his feet Lord. Eliminate his fears of "becoming" like his dad, Lord. Lord Protect him from the weight of not feeling good enough to be a husband or a father. Lord, I pray that you enter every empty space. Speak to the little boy yearning for love on the inside of him. Lord, I pray that you remind him that he is fearfully *and* wonderfully made. Tell him that the only shoes he has to fill are his own. Lord keep him steady, stable, and not stagnant. Let him be a man of his word. Lord, build up integrity on the inside of him. I speak healing over his hurts and his fears that have influenced him from childhood to manhood. I speak life into this man right now in the name of Jesus. I do not care what lies the enemy has told him about himself— remind him of your truth. Lord, I am thankful that even in our mess, you still call us your own. I call this man healed, delivered, and set free from everything that has tried to take him out. I speak to his mental health right now in the name of Jesus, and I pray that you keep and cover his mind. Lord, let his mind rest in you. Give him a peace that surpasses *all* understanding.

Verse: *"I have told you these things, so that in me you may have peace, In this world you will have trouble. But take heart! I have overcome the world." (John 16:33 NIV)*

COVER HIM

_____

_____

_____

_____

_____

_____

_____

_____

_____

_____

_____

_____

_____

_____

_____

_____

_____

_____

_____

COVER HIM

_____

_____

_____

_____

_____

_____

_____

_____

_____

_____

_____

_____

_____

_____

_____

_____

_____

_____

_____

CHAPTER 5

HEALTH TO HIS NAVEL

Affirmation: "My husband will have control over his flesh."

A Prayer for My Husband's Health

God, I thank you that you breathed breath into our bodies and created us in your image. Lord, I pray that we never take your creation, your image nor your likeness for granted. I pray right now for my husband's body. I pray that he is walking in optimal health in the name of Jesus. God, I speak against sickness and disease right now, and decree and declare long life to him. Longevity shall be his portion. Lord, I pray that all his vital organs will continue to function to their greatest capacity. I release a healing anointing right now over my husband in the name of Jesus. Lord, maximize his strength and his endurance. I pray that he can be disciplined in what he consumes and allows into his temple. Lord, I speak against predisposed illnesses right now. Whatever diseases that have run rampant in his bloodline stops NOW! It stops here. Lord, I speak against the spirit of addiction right now in the name of Jesus. Set my husband free from any addictive traits right now, Jesus. Allow my husband to be fruitful in the earth realm. I speak to his reproductive organs right now in the name of Jesus. I pray that every seed he has will have the ability to produce a healthy child. My husband will have Abraham's anointing in Jesus' name, Amen.

Verse: *"They will soar on wings like eagles; they will run and not grow weary; they will walk and not faint." (Isaiah 40:31 NIV)*

COVER HIM

_____

_____

_____

_____

_____

_____

_____

_____

_____

_____

_____

_____

_____

_____

_____

_____

_____

_____

_____

_____

_____

_____

_____

_____

_____

_____

_____

_____

_____

_____

_____

_____

_____

_____

_____

_____

CHAPTER 6

ANOINTING IS HIS PORTION

*Affirmation: "My husband is anointed
and called by God."*

A Prayer for My Husband's Spiritual Well-Being

Dear God, I cover my husband's spiritual well-being right now. I pray that you would anoint his head with oil, and allow the oil to flow. Allow it to flow from the top of his head to the soles of his feet. Lord, I pray that he will proclaim your gospel, unashamed, to all he encounters. Let his life be a living, breathing, walking testimony of your favor, grace, and goodness. I pray Lord God for the ministry that is in him. Allow his ministry to come forth in the name of Jesus. Let him not die with his giftings and callings, Lord. Allow him to pursue the calling you have placed on his life. Lord, I pray that you baptize him right now with your Holy Spirit. Let him know you on a greater and deeper level, Lord. I pray that you bless him with spiritual gifts according to your will and desires for his life. Lord, allow him to see in the spirit, to hear your voice clearly, so that he may be led by your voice and not by his own vision(s) for his life. Lord, bring him in alignment with your word, and let it be a lamp unto his feet and a light unto his path. Illuminate your word as he studies the scriptures, and let it illuminate in his life. Lord, may your Holy Spirit come alive through him, setting him afire in the name of Jesus. Give him a prayer posture. Lord, let him enjoy resting in your presence and glory in worship. Teach him how to walk by faith and not by sight. Teach him to always seek you *first* in every plan, decision, and at every roadblock. It's in Jesus' name I pray, Amen.

Verse: *"Blessed is the one who does not walk in the counsel of the ungodly or stand in the way that sinners take or sit in the company of mockers, but whose delight is in the law of the Lord, and who meditates on his law day and night. That person is like a tree planted by streams of water, which yields its fruit in season and whose leaf does not wither, whatever they do prospers." (Psalms 1:1-3 NIV)*

COVER HIM

_____

_____

_____

_____

_____

_____

_____

_____

_____

_____

_____

_____

_____

_____

_____

_____

_____

_____

_____

COVER HIM

_____

_____

_____

_____

_____

_____

_____

_____

_____

_____

_____

_____

_____

_____

_____

_____

_____

_____

_____

CHAPTER 7

BE THY SERVANT

Affirmation: "My husband has a divine purpose on this earth."

A Prayer for My Husband's Purpose

Lord, you know the plans that you have for my husband, allow him to operate in them. Should there be any uncertainty in his heart regarding his purpose, I pray you may bring clarity to him. I pray that he knows and understands why you have called him and why you chose him. Lord, allow him to walk confidently in the things of you. Lord, let him walk boldly in his calling and his purpose. I pray right now against any attack of the enemy that has been set out to deter my husband from his purpose. I ask that you cancel every assignment of the enemy meant to keep him from walking out his God given purpose. Lord I cancel every lie of the enemy that's tried to tell my husband that he is unworthy and that you can't use him. Lord remind him of every promise that you have for him. Remind him that the blood shed on the cross for him has redeemed him and has allowed him to start anew. I speak against the spirit of fear that may be holding him back from his calling. I call my husband forth right now in the name of Jesus:

_____

(Insert Name)

Come forth right now! Come forth right now! You have been predestined for this; you are built for this. It's time you answer. Stop being afraid, step out on faith. Receive it now in the name of Jesus, amen.

COVER HIM

_____

_____

_____

_____

_____

_____

_____

_____

_____

_____

_____

_____

_____

_____

_____

_____

_____

_____

_____

_____

_____

_____

_____

_____

_____

_____

_____

_____

_____

_____

_____

_____

_____

_____

_____

_____

_____

CHAPTER 8

COMFORT IN YOUR CORRECTION

*Affirmation: "My husband is an
amazing and patient father."*

A Prayer for My Husband's Parenting

Lord, I thank you that when you created my husband, you created him to be the head of our family. I also thank you that when you created him you also created him with the ability to father a generation. Lord, I thank you that my husband is a great father. I thank you that he will influence and impact our children and every child connected to him in Jesus' name. Lord, I pray that you give him the strength and compassion to be a good father. I pray to the Lord that you teach him how to love and nurture our children in such a way that they will grow confidently in their father's love. I pray that our children will cherish and respect his authority. Lord, I ask that you teach him how to be sensitive to their needs and when to administer discipline for correction. Lord, I pray that you would guide him into fatherhood and give him the grace he needs to not only manage being a father, but to execute his role as a mentor to generations. I pray that you continue to gift him the tools and resources needed to pour into generations. Help him to be a role model and inspiration to children who have no fathers and no guidance in their homes, Lord. Let him be a magnet to attract young men seeking a good father figure and someone to love. Give him the strength to balance his giftings in this role and grace him to maintain healthy relationships with those whom he pours into. I ask these things in Jesus' name, amen.

Verse: *These commandments that I give you are to be on your hearts. Impress them on your children. Talk about them when you sit at home and when you walk along the road, when you lie down and when you wake up." (Deuteronomy 6: 6-7 NIV)*

_____

_____

_____

_____

_____

_____

_____

_____

_____

_____

_____

_____

_____

_____

_____

_____

_____

_____

_____

COVER HIM

_____

_____

_____

_____

_____

_____

_____

_____

_____

_____

_____

_____

_____

_____

_____

_____

_____

_____

_____

CHAPTER 9

A GODLY SUBMISSION

*Affirmation: "My husband will lead
like Christ led the church"*

A Prayer for My Husband's Leadership

Lord, I thank you for my husband's position. I thank you that he will come along and be the leader of our family. Lord, I pray that as he walks in his divine purpose in this marriage, he takes pride in his efforts to love, counsel, and lead his family. I pray Lord that even when it gets hard, when he doesn't feel like "showing up", that he draws strength from you Lord and continues to push through into his calling. Lord teach me how to be a good helpmeet that supports and nurtures my husband's role. Help me to never tear him down, but build him up so he can be the best man he needs to be on this earth and for our family. Lord, I pray that right now, you would begin to build his character for leadership. Lord let honesty and integrity flow through him. I pray he builds his foundation on wisdom and trust. God, I pray that as he seeks validation for decisions regarding his family, that he is led by you. I pray he seeks you with all of his heart, mind, soul, and strength. Lord, I pray that when the enemy revolts against him that you would create a standard in him and give him the power to combat the enemy. Lord, I pray that my husband would use his weapons of prayer to cover our family, to war in the spirit and to rebuke every devourer that comes up against our family in Jesus' name, amen.

Verse: *"Submit to one another out of reverence for Christ. Wives, submit yourselves to your husbands as you do to the Lord. For the husband is the head of the wife as Christ is the head of the church, his body, of which he is the Savior."* *(Ephesians 5: 21-23 NIV)*

_____

_____

_____

_____

_____

_____

_____

_____

_____

_____

_____

_____

_____

_____

_____

_____

_____

_____

_____

_____

_____

_____

_____

_____

_____

_____

_____

_____

_____

_____

_____

_____

_____

_____

_____

_____

CHAPTER 10

UNBREAKABLE COVENANT

*Affirmation: "My husband will cherish
and choose me daily"*

A Prayer for My Husband Fidelity and Commitment

Lord, I cover my husband right now in the name of Jesus. I pray against any spirit of lust that may be creeping in on his walk in purity. Lord, I pray that he can honor his commitment to you, because I know if he can honor the commitment he's made to you, then he will have no issues honoring the covenant between the two of us. I pray against masturbation and pornography right now in the name of Jesus. Lord, I pray conviction falls on him heavily in this area. Allow him to recognize the importance of this season right now as he begins to walk in purity. Lord, I pray that he commits his heart, mind, thoughts, and body to you and you alone. I pray that he is preparing himself for a healthy, committed relationship.

Lord, I speak against the spirit of divorce and division right now in the name of Jesus. I pray that my husband has a tenacity to declare that we will have a healthy, prosperous marriage. I pray that he will begin, even now, to choose me and will continue to choose me each and every day of our lives. Teach him how to be disciplined in his spirit and in his flesh. Lord, I speak against fleshful tendencies and vulnerabilities. Lord search his heart, if there should be anything lingering that may sabotage his walk, I pray that you remove it right now in the name of Jesus, Amen.

Verse: Husbands, in the same way be considerate as you live with your wives and treat them with respect as the weaker partner and as heirs with you of the gracious gift of life, so that nothing will hinder your prayers. (1 Peter 3:7 NIV)

_____

_____

_____

_____

_____

_____

_____

_____

_____

_____

_____

_____

_____

_____

_____

_____

_____

_____

_____

_____

_____

_____

_____

_____

_____

_____

_____

_____

_____

_____

_____

_____

_____

_____

_____

_____

_____

_____

_____

CHAPTER 11

LOVE THY NEIGHBOR

*Affirmation: My husband will maintain
and sustain healthy relationships"*

A Prayer for My Husband's Relationships

Lord, I pray for my husband's current relationships and past relationships. I pray that you reveal and fill every void area of his past relationships that may have left him seeking answers and validation. I rebuke every strong-hold and every soul tie that may be attached to him. I pray a release happens suddenly, unexpectedly, right now Jesus! I pray he can be free from the bondage of every stronghold that was ever present in his life. We cancel it right now. I pray healing over his relationship with him and his parents. I pray he finds strength to confront his hidden hurts head-on with respect and humility. Lord, I pray against any feelings of abandonment, rejection, or resentment that may be lingering from those relationships. I pray that you strengthen his relationships with his friends and give him a community of other believers who can encourage and support him in his walk with you God. I thank you that he values relationships with people. I pray he can find balance with maintaining healthy boundaries within these relationships. Teach him how to communicate his desires as well as his feelings towards his peers. Lord, encourage my husband to step outside of his comfort zone when it comes with building relationships with other people. Most importantly God, I pray for his relationship with you, let it be whole and purposeful. Lord, I pray that he can learn to lean, trust, and depend on you. I pray you fill him up and overwhelm him with your love and your protection in Jesus' name, amen.

Verse: *"Love the Lord your God with all your heart and with all your soul and with all your mind. This is the first and greatest commandment. And the second is like it; Love your neighbor as yourself." (Matthew 22:37-39 NIV)*

_____

_____

_____

_____

_____

_____

_____

_____

_____

_____

_____

_____

_____

_____

_____

_____

_____

_____

_____

CHAPTER 12

OPERATING IN WHOLENESS

*Affirmation: "My husband will serve
God's kingdom boldly"*

A Prayer for My Husband's Church Hurt

Lord, I pray against any offense that may have occurred in the church involving my husband. I pray against any misrepresentation or gossip that resulted after this offense. God, I pray for healing and complete restoration for anything my husband may have experienced at the hands of "church people." I pray those same people will have open hearts to receive the appropriate conviction. I pray they are led by your spirit and not by the tactics and lies of the enemy. I speak against any wolf in sheep's clothing that may come to disrupt the flow of the spirit amongst God's people and in his holy sanctuary. I pray for my husband's discernment and that you may reveal those individuals who are not in his best interest. Lord remove and replace as you see fit. I pray he finds a church home that is filled with love and harmony among believers. I pray that this offense or hurt doesn't keep him from worshiping among the congregation. I also ask that you may heal his heart towards "man" and remind him that the same grace you showed him, you expect him to show to others. I believe it so, even now in Jesus' name, amen.

Verse: *Bear with each other and forgive one another if any of you has a grievance against someone. Forgive as the Lord forgave you." (Colossians 3:13 NIV)*

_____

_____

_____

_____

_____

_____

_____

_____

_____

_____

_____

_____

_____

_____

_____

_____

_____

_____

CHAPTER 13

LET IT BE PLEASING

*Affirmation: "My husband will
only desire me"*

A Prayer for My Husband's Intimacy

Lord, I pray that my husband only has desires for me. I pray that his eyes will be fixed on me. Lord, I thank you that my husband will be faithful to me and me alone. I pray for a deeper level of intimacy in the name of Jesus. Lord, I'm believing that the sex will be beautiful and amazing. Teach my husband how to please me and satisfy my sexual desires. Let not our marriage bed be defiled. Teach us how to have passionate love. Teach us how to work towards intimacy in our everyday lives. Lord, I'm believing for my husband to be affectionate, caring, thoughtful, selfless, spontaneous, and supportive. Lord, I pray that he places our needs above his own; in return Lord, teach me how to make him a priority. Lord,

I pray that my husband makes it easy to serve and submit to him. Let it be my reasonable service because of how he shows up in our family. Lord, I pray that my husband will love me out loud. I pray that he will always think of new and creative ways to show his love for me. I thank you that he will always choose me in Jesus' name, amen.

Verse: *"Marriage should be honored by all, and the marriage bed kept pure, for God will judge the sexually immoral."* *(Hebrews 13:4 NIV)*

Made in the USA
Columbia, SC
19 April 2022

59093300R00048